EVERYTHING I NEEDED TO KNOW ABOUT SUCCEEDING IN HOLLYWOOD I LEARNED FROM MY PIT-BULL

by David Chasman

DOVE
BOOKS

A
HOLLYWOOD
HANDBOOK

CAREER GUIDE
AND
POCKET COMPANION

THINGS THEY DON'T
TEACH YOU
IN FILM SCHOOL

THINGS THAT
TRANSAMERICA, COCA-COLA,
SONY AND MATSUSHITA
DIDN'T KNOW
BUT LATER FOUND OUT

THINGS THAT
SEAGRAM
WILL SOON DISCOVER

ISBN 0-7871-0492-2

Printed in the United States of America

Dove Books
301 North Cañon Drive
Beverly Hills, CA 90210

Distributed by Penguin USA

Text layout by Carolyn Wendt
Cover design by David Chasman and Rick Penn-Kraus

First Printing: August, 1995

10 9 8 7 6 5 4 3 2 1

For Johanna and Rebecca

Author's Note:

When, in reading this text, you encounter nouns like "man," "men," "star," "actor," "executive," "writer," "producer," "director," "agent," or "egomaniac," followed by pronouns like "he," "him," or "his," be assured that—in accordance with traditional English usage—the observation pertains to both the male and female of the species.

At the insistence of the publisher, the author has supplied the following biographical information, which he describes as his "rap sheet":

David Chasman was educated, if that is the word, at the School of Industrial Art in New York and the Académie de la Grande-Chaumière in Paris.

Before achieving penury in the movie business, he supported himself in luxurious fashion working as a cartoonist, caricaturist, illustrator, set designer, graphic designer, *affichiste,* main-title designer, record sleeve designer, book illustrator, art director and copywriter.

As United Artists' executive advertising director in New York, he created the ad campaigns for more than a hundred films, including *The Apartment, Tom Jones, West Side Story, Judgment at Nuremburg, It's a Mad Mad Mad Mad World, Dr. No, Irma La Douce, From Russia with Love, Goldfinger, Never on Sunday, Elmer Gantry, The Manchurian Candidate, The Alamo, A Hard Day's Night* and the *Pink Panther* movies.

As production head for United Artists in London, he was charged with supervising—and managed not to impede—the making of some 110 films including the James Bond pictures *Thunderball, You Only Live Twice,* and *Live and Let Die,* the Beatles' movie *Help!, Women in Love, The Whisperers,*

*A Funny Thing Happened on the Way to the Forum,
The Train, Kes* and *The Charge of the Light Brigade.*

In America, as executive vice president in charge
of production at, successively, United Artists,
Columbia Pictures, and Metro-Goldwyn-Mayer, he
artfully contrived not to obstruct the making of
*Midnight Cowboy, Diamonds Are Forever, Live and
Let Die, Hospital, Last Tango in Paris,* the Woody
Allen films *Bananas, Sleeper,* and *Everything You
Wanted to Know about Sex, Stir Crazy, Poltergeist*
and *Pennies from Heaven.*

He has produced one television movie, *Murder
on Flight 502,* and executive produced two theatrical
features, *Brighton Beach Memoirs* and *The Secret of
My Success,* for a lifetime batting average of .666!

He maintains his greatest career distinction is
that he is the only production executive employed at
Columbia Pictures between 1977 and 1980 who had
absolutely nothing to do with the making of *Kramer
vs. Kramer.*

THE ART OF FILM

The greatest testimonial to the vitality of the art of film is that, for a hundred years, it has survived the best efforts of the businessmen to kill it.

"There is no such thing as a good script," was said in all seriousness by the great John Ford. This will give you a fair idea of how directors feel about writers.

"Write me a story on the same lines of *Blind Husbands*," was said to a writer in all seriousness by the great Irving Thalberg. This will give you a fair idea of how studio executives feel about writers.

"I can't speak these lines! This dialogue is pure shit!" was said by the great Margaret Sullavan upon reading F. Scott Fitzgerald's script for *Three Comrades*. This will give you a fair idea of how actors feel about writers.

"Writing is a profession in which you have to keep proving your talent to people who have none," was said by the great French essayist Jules Renard. This will give you a fair idea of how writers feel about directors, executives and actors.

The actors who can speak most eloquently on the subject of great screen acting are seldom the actors who can do it.

If the ability to simulate foreign accents had anything to do with great acting, Chico Marx would have brought home an Academy Award.

Despite conspicuous evidence to the contrary, bad manners are *not* an essential component of filmmaking talent.

Since the night Thespis did his first walk-on, there has never been—and there never will be—an actor who could not recite *verbatim* the worst review he ever got.

Most dramatic plots—like most people—are, when stripped to their underwear, ridiculous.

In writing a film script (or a play, for that matter), construction is the last refuge of hacks.

In Hollywood, professional compliments are often rather sneaky forms of self-congratulation.

In the immediate afterglow of a huge box office hit you can hear effusive appreciations from

Writers:
"He's a great producer! He didn't change one word of my script!"

Actors:
"A wonderful director! He gave me a free hand!"

Directors:
"Superb actress! Takes direction beautifully!"

Producers:
"I want to thank the many talented people who contributed to the realization of my dream!"

Executives:
"A lot of credit should go to my loyal staff, who sat with me for eight days and nights after the first rough cut, helping me to whip the picture into shape!"

Screenwriting *can* be an art, but virtually all screen-writers are artisans, manufacturing screenplays according to plans and specifications laid down by other people—usually idiots.

The quality in a writer which studio executives prize most highly is docility—possibly because it is the only literary attribute they are equipped to recognize.

A writer once put it, "The studio asked for changes, some of which I agreed to and all of which I made."

In film, as in literature or theater, the smash hit comforts and celebrates; the work of art confronts and disturbs.

To allow himself to fall in love with the art of film is tragic in a studio executive.

It requires an extraordinary amount of ability to make even a very bad film.

The word which describes a man making films to please only himself is the same word which describes a man making love only to himself.

The legendary Ben Hecht wrote: "Of the three thousand screenwriters in Hollywood, there are barely fifty men and women of talent. But the work of the fifty is indistinguishable from the rest, because we all have to toe the same mark." This should be remembered by studio executives whenever they are tempted to provide a writer with "input."

Directing a film is the general process of introducing novelty into a system of interacting variables.

The average studio executive genuinely believes that paying somebody to write or direct or produce a film is the same thing as doing it himself—that is, if we're talking about hits. When it comes to flops, the separation of functions is rigidly observed.

Filmmakers seldom wish other filmmakers well.

In Hollywood, no news is bad news.

Let me tell you something about how studio executives relate to movies:

They have no love for the art; they have no respect for the craft; they have no grasp of the business; they have no knowledge of its history; they have no feeling for what it is that audiences want out of movies.

Are there exceptions to this melancholy rule? Yes.

But not enough to make a significant statistical difference.

The studio executive who starts out by saying, "Let me be perfectly honest with you," is usually about to tell a lie.

A scene which is believable but not possible is better, in a film, than a scene which is possible but not believable.

The basis of all dramatic criticism is the unspoken assumption that the critics are wiser than the creators.

"The wisest of critics is an altering being, subject to the better insight of the morrow," observed William James.

When panning a film (which they have just seen), critics routinely indict the script (which they have never read). Critics should know that what gets shot is not necessarily what was written. Ask any screenwriter.

Anatole France wrote: "The good critic is he who relates the adventures of his soul among masterpieces." The infrequency of film masterpieces and the sparseness of sensitive souls may account for the conspicuous scarcity of good film critics.

Once a studio executive has finished reading a script, it is difficult to persuade him that the improvements which occur to him in the first five minutes did not also occur to the writer in the first five minutes.

Here's the studio executive problem in a nutshell: genius recognizes genius; talent recognizes talent; but mediocrity knows nothing higher than itself.

Most studio executives are simply not equipped to render literary judgments, script evaluations, or talent assessments. They know only how to *accept established reputations.*

When a project is turned down, the reasons given by the studio executive are almost never the *real* reasons.

Beware of the executive who gives detailed notes on script revisions. He will hotly deny ever having done so, if the results fail to please his superiors.

"The son-of-a-bitch let us down! We need a fresh new writer," is the usual line.

On the other hand, if the changes should happen to meet with the superiors' approval, the dialogue goes like this:

"I had to sit with him every night and practically give it to him line by line!"

Able studio executives (there *are* a handful) recognize that they should function as gentle midwives to the birth of movies. The majority, however, are preoccupied with desperate attempts to associate themselves with hits, distance themselves from flops and, in general, echo the opinions of their superiors in the studio pecking order.

In the savagely competitive arena of Hollywood filmmaking, failures have very few friends. Successes have no friends at all—just hangers-on.

Old-time medicine shows hired entertainers to attract big crowds. Modern politicians exploit movie stars for the same purpose.

Often, this association persuades the movie stars to make public pronouncements on national policy —motivated, apparently, by the curious belief that selling the snake oil is more dignified than playing the banjo.

An astute observer said: "On a movie set, the director is God—unfortunately, the actors are atheists!"

In 1934, in a movie called *It Happened One Night,* Clark Gable removed his shirt and was seen to be bare to the waist. In the next twelve months, the sale of men's undershirts dropped a ruinous 35 percent.

In 1939, for a movie called *Gone with the Wind,* costume designer Walter Plunkett revived a Civil War era hair net called a snood. For the next six years—all through World War II—the women of America wore snoods by the millions.

These events were calmly recognized by the motion picture industry as evidence of the enormous power of the screen to influence audiences.

For the past half-century, those same audiences have watched John Wayne, James Cagney, Gary Cooper, Alan Ladd, Clint Eastwood, Sly Stallone and Arnold Schwarzenegger resolve any and every conceivable human conflict by the simple expedient of murdering somebody.

Or a lot of somebodies.

Our society is now engulfed by a climate of violence wherein murder is seen—and applauded—as the only acceptable method of settling social disagreement and political difference, and of affirming manliness and personal dignity.

The motion picture industry demurely maintains that, in this instance, the screen has no power whatever to influence audiences about anything.

The Motion Picture Producers Association rating system's nonchalance toward violence is exceeded only by its priggishness toward sex—and its hypocrisy toward practically everything.

This paradox was neatly summarized by Jack Nicholson: "If you hack off a woman's breast with a meat ax, it's a PG. But if you kiss it, it's an NC-17."

Tendencies to maudlin self-pity, insane egotism, bottomless folly and hysterical mendacity make acting an ideal profession for certain persons who, for all other constructive social purposes, would be quite useless.

In Hollywood, any raging egomaniac who wields enough power to tyrannize everybody in the immediate vicinity is described as "a perfectionist"—as if his every transient, half-assed, lunatic whim represented some immutable criterion of flawlessness.

Somebody really brilliant once said, "Every actor, however modest, keeps a most outrageous vanity chained like a madman in the padded cell of his breast."

Narcissism is to actors what silicosis is to coal miners.

The occupational disease of studio executives is simultanagnosia.*

---

* The inability to comprehend more than one element of a visual scene at the same time or to integrate the parts as a whole.—*Dorland's Medical Dictionary*

You are an actor because of your ability to submerge yourself in a role that you play. You are a star because of the part of you that won't submerge.

We are all of us fundamentally actors, in that we cherish delusional views of our own talents and we continue to cast ourselves in parts for which we are no longer—if we ever were—suitable.

Somerset Maugham said it: "I have never met an author who admitted that people did not buy his work because it was dull." He might have added, "—or a filmmaker."

There is not an actor in the world—or, for that matter, a director, producer, screenwriter, editor, cinematographer, composer, designer, technician or film school undergraduate—who does not have tucked away somewhere, in a notebook or a drawer or a corner of his mind, the first draft of an Academy Award acceptance speech.

The Academy was formed in 1927 to "advance the arts and sciences of motion pictures and to foster cooperation among the creative leadership of the industry for cultural, educational and technological progress."

Almost as an afterthought did they decide to recognize outstanding filmmaking achievements by the presentation of annual Awards of Merit.

The Academy could not have foreseen that, in so doing, they were creating the entire self-congratulation industry.

In conferring its annual Awards of Merit, the Academy of Motion Picture Arts and Sciences has frequently been the target of indignant censure and peevish criticism for its nominating procedures.

It is a curious fact that, in the sixty-eight years of the Academy's history, not one protest has ever been registered by a nominee.

Perhaps the greatest disadvantage of superstardom is the fact that the star must spend 99 percent of his time exclusively in the company of persons who have a direct financial interest in kissing his ass. There is simply no one within his range of hearing who ever says to him, "That is the *dumbest* idea I ever heard in my life!"

The pressure of this unrelenting compliance can disturb even the most rock-solid equilibrium or warp the keenest judgment.

And superstars are not renowned for either quality.

One of the common maladies which afflicts Hollywood people who have achieved great success—and fame and wealth and the power that comes with it—is the clinical delusion that they are automatically entitled to a laudatory press.

And that when they don't get it, it is only because the writer is unqualified, unfair, biased, malicious and, probably, in the pay of jealous and vindictive rivals.

Avoid books with titles like *Selling Your Film Script, How to Market Your Screenplay* and *Secrets of Successful Screenwriting*. If their authors knew anything about selling film scripts that was worth knowing, they wouldn't be writing books. They would be selling film scripts.

H. G. Wells clearly had intimate knowledge of film producers and studio executives when he wrote: "No passion in the world is equal to the passion to alter someone else's draft."

With the possible exception of the floor of the United States Congress, there is no spot on earth where you can hear more bullshit spoken than the lobby of an American theater showing a subtitled foreign film.

Many in Hollywood derive hope, strength and spiritual sustenance from other people's flops.

Recently, a group of highly accomplished filmmakers were commiserating with each other on the discouraging condition of the movie business in general and, in particular, on their recent commercial failures. One observed, "You know, if it wasn't for the people we hate—there wouldn't be any hits at all!"

There are two valid reasons why movie people are usually fearful of press interviews. The first is that they might be misquoted; the second is that they might be quoted accurately.

Movie stars discussing their exhaustive researches in preparation for a role, producers reporting their opening-day grosses, and studio executives describing their intimate involvement with the making of a blockbuster hit are not testifying under oath.

For the great majority of Hollywood people, working in movies bears an amazing resemblance to unemployment.

The power of a superstar is not mystical: it has a sound economic basis. A superstar decides he likes a script and, suddenly, two hundred people have well-paying jobs—lasting from three months to two years.

In the entire history of talking pictures, there has never been a character actor so ill-favored by nature that he could not see himself playing romantic leads. "Look at Spencer Tracy!" is the refrain.

All theatrical film, all drama, all fiction—and, possibly, life itself—consists of variations on a handful of plots.

THE MOVIE BUSINESS

There is no *businesslike* show business!

Before giant corporate entities like Transamerica, Sony, Coca-Cola and Matsushita were able to grasp this fundamental truth, they had pissed away billions of dollars and endured indescribable vexation.

The production and distribution of motion pictures makes betting on horses seem like a solid, low-risk, predictable business.

Much mischief has resulted from our persistent habit of referring to ourselves as an "industry." We are nothing of the kind. There is no repetitive industrial pattern in the manufacture of our product; there are no objective, mensurable criteria of excellence in our product. The two great Shibboleths of the Wharton School, quality control and cost control, have no practical application to the fabrication of our product. Nobody ever went to see a movie because it was made efficiently.

What are we, then? We are a conjunction of high art, cottage handicrafts and a floating crap game. Whatever that is, it's not an industry.

In the production and distribution of movies, all decision is in response to the perceived instruction of the marketplace.

This being the case, why does every company, without exception, go to such lengths to distort—if not downright *falsify*—the information that the marketplace yields? Studios are invariably coy about how much a film cost and routinely mendacious about how much a film earned.

Consequently, their decisions are in response to the perceived instruction of their own bullshit.

Sentimental, amorphous drama; coarse, pointless comedy; steamy eroticism; rough force in action; these have been the commercial mainstays of show business for four thousand years—to the abject despair of anyone aspiring to a performing art with any brains in it.

Most of the producers in Hollywood and—with a few exceptions—*all* of the studio executives are, at best, brokers in other people's creativity. This is not a shameful way to make a living, but it's nothing to get all puffed-up about, either.

In the baroque logic of modern Hollywood, the studio considers that someone who has produced four consecutive flops is a safer bet than someone who has yet to produce a film.

The producer of *six* consecutive flops is frequently hired to run the studio.

Movies are the only business in which the opinion of the man who invests $40 million can be contradicted with impunity by the opinion of the man who invests seven dollars and fifty cents.

No studio head should ever expect to hear hard truths from anybody who's looking for a three-picture deal.

Private screening rooms can be dangerously misleading. The people who go to the movies are different from the people who have movies brought to them. There is nothing like a trip to the local movie house to determine what audiences *really* think of what's up there on the screen.

To function successfully, a production head requires a faculty of intuition which is almost mystical in character. So abstruse is the nature of this faculty, that it is called "genius" by sycophants, "luck" by rivals and "competent management" by Wall Street.

Running a studio is like leading a cavalry charge. The position is prominent, but the mortality rate is unnervingly high.

The majority of studio executives (like the majority of people anywhere) are not merely incapable of creativity—they resent it furiously. To them, a wit is someone who is laughing at them.

After a sneak preview, nobody connected with the movie—repeat, *nobody*—wants your honest opinion. Do not be deluded into thinking that there are any exceptions to this rule. The studio did not spend $60 million to provide you with an occasion to demonstrate your integrity.

Disinterested enthusiasm is seldom encountered in Hollywood. What they call "smog" is, in reality, the noxious miasma arising from the dust and din of a million axes grinding.

You get three chances to make a movie great. The first is when writing the script. The second is when shooting it. The third—and best—chance is in the editing.

Of course, if you can't raise the money—you get no chances at all.

In the Orthodox Religion of Hollywood, the smash hit is our ultimate epiphany.

The vast sums which studios spend on market research enable them to confidently predict that audiences will turn out for hits and stay away from flops.

Research is neither a science nor a religion; it is a tool—and a frequently misused tool, at that.

You know how the Ford Motor Company blew 25 percent of its net worth on the Edsel? Research.

Research—questionnaires, interviews, surveys, trials—can only provide a data base, nothing more. In other words, you get a set of facts—*from which other facts may be inferred*. Your "research" is only as valuable as the shrewdness and accuracy of the inferences you draw from your data base.

Incompetent marketing people (they comprise the majority) use research much the way a drunk uses the corner lamppost: for support, instead of illumination.

Consider this example:

In launching its disastrous New Coke, the Coca-Cola Company spent staggering amounts of money conducting blindfold taste tests. From the data base the tests provided, they inferred that New Coke would outperform not only the competition, but the original Coke as well.

From the same data base, what they *should* have inferred is that practically nobody drinks blindfolded.

Before a film's release, studios are seldom candid in marketing discussions with filmmakers. The only way a producer can tell what the marketing people really think is by listening to the pronouns. If the marketers say "our" movie, they think it's a hit. If they say "your" movie—*look out!*

It is true that Griffith, Murnau, Lubitsch, Ford and their contemporaries were denied the advantages of today's miraculous film technologies. On the other hand, they never had to hear about focus groups, either.

Niccolò Machiavelli would have had a brilliant career in Hollywood. What he wrote of a sixteenth-century prince is equally true of a twentieth-century studio head: "The first method for estimating his intelligence is to look at the men he has around him."

In Hollywood, an "independent" producer is a man who blows soap bubbles and pretends that they're bowling balls. The miracle is that, every now and then, one of them knocks over a few pins!

In order to prosper, what studios *need* to run them are skilled professionals at understanding great talent, great stories, and mercurial audience tastes. What studios *get* to run them are skilled professionals at ass-kissing, credit-grabbing and self-promotion.

With very rare exceptions, most men and women become studio executives as the last refuge of general incompetence.

The sheer *number* of production executives at the average studio is an industry joke. They should fire half of them for a start. If history is any guide, they will fire the *wrong* half—but even that would be an improvement.

The cross that the independent producer bears is this: he must expend the major portion of his time eagerly —tirelessly—*desperately*—soliciting the approval of executives whose mental capacity he despises.

Readers in studio story departments do not read submitted manuscripts with any great care. They are more concerned with career politicking than with perceptive literary analysis (assuming they are capable of it in the first place).

The ideal movie executive has a perception of the audience that is unclouded by intellect, undisturbed by conscience, unencumbered by taste and untroubled by a sense of social responsibility.

"Humankind cannot bear very much reality," so said T. S. Eliot. For people planning a production schedule, this is a valuable lesson to learn.

The production and distribution contracts that producers sign with studios contain strict requirements for the length of a movie, but make no provision whatever for its breadth or its depth.

The power to alter a screenplay is not the same thing as the talent to improve it.

The movie business and the art of film are separate subjects for discussion but, like the human body and the human soul, they are inextricably linked. The health of one is directly dependent upon the health of the other.

You will not be capable of lofty, poetic thoughts if your digestion is rotten; the art of film cannot achieve new aesthetic heights if the movie business is dying at the box office.

An agent's effectiveness stems from his ability to persuade people to take him at his own evaluation.

There are no powerful agents. No film ever halted production because the agent failed to show up.

There *are* agents with powerful clients. But all power is ephemeral, and when the client's power fades, the agent—rather than fade with him—gets a new client.

The *lingua franca* of agentry is bullshit. But studio heads *understand* bullshit—and speak it fluently.

The conventional agent mentality is best expressed as follows: if it happens—*they* succeeded; if it doesn't happen—*you* failed.

"Let every eye negotiate for itself and trust no agent," grumbles Claudio in *Much Ado about Nothing.*

"O world, world, world! Thus is the poor agent despis'd," moans Pandarus when everybody bad-mouths him in *Troilus and Cressida*. But he goes on to say, "Why should our endeavor be so desir'd, and the performance so loath'd?"

"Then came each actor on his ass," observes Hamlet.

Shakespeare understood show business.

It is the responsibility of the studio head to hire the best talent he can at the lowest possible price. It is the obligation of the agent to get jobs for whatever talent he represents at the highest possible price.

The qualities that studio heads look for in an agent are modesty, timidity and subservience. The qualities that agents desire most in a studio head are credulousness, ignorance and tractability.

It is, therefore, both clear and logical that studio heads and agents are natural adversaries and bitter antagonists.

So why, in the name of common sense, does a conglomerateur, seeking a studio head for his newly purchased movie studio, consult an *agent* for suggestions? Exactly what sort of executive does he think the agent is going to recommend?

In Hollywood, betrayal is the rule; loyalty is the exception.

The delusion which is epidemic among young waiters in Hollywood restaurants is that, when they finally get an acting job, it will be a step up.

If audiences were really interested in their own betterment and instruction, they could attend church for free, rather than part with hard cash to see a movie.

In the professional jargon of movie-making, actors, writers, directors and their auxiliaries are classified as "talent."

Studio executives regard talent much as electricians regard light bulbs. They know the lamp is useless without them. They know also that light bulbs burn out. And when they *do* burn out, they are discarded—and promptly replaced with new ones.

And it was the critic St. John Irvine who aptly noted: "No one can fully appreciate the fatuity of human nature until he has spent some time in a box office."

When studio executives talk about a "good" film, it's not always clear what it is that they mean. G. K. Chesterton once wrote: "The word 'good' has many meanings. For example, if a man were to shoot his grandmother at a range of five hundred yards, I should call him a good shot—but not *necessarily* a good man."

Asking the producer of a mega-hit movie to explain its success is much like asking a lottery winner to expound on John Maynard Keynes' *Inductive Use of Statistical Frequencies for the Determination of Probability.*

From its very beginnings, the movie business has been an arena where "too old" is a serious obstacle to employment, but "too dumb" is not. This is either a sad fact, or a cheerful one—depending on where your interests lie.

Genuine talent is so hard to come by in filmmaking, that no studio can afford to be finicky about the race, the religion, the gender, the age, the ethnicity, the politics, the sexual preferences or even the *amiability* of the body in which the talent is contained.

Next time you feel inclined to grumble about the extravagant compensations being thrown about in Hollywood, remember that Michael Eisner and Steven Spielberg and Cruise and Katzenberg and Schwarzenegger and Stallone—and you and I and the guy at the car wash—all work for *exactly the same salary*: as much as we can get.

Sébastien-Roch-Nicolas Chamfort was talking about eighteenth-century France, but his description sounds remarkably like twentieth-century Hollywood: "...a country where it is often helpful to advertise your vices—and always dangerous to demonstrate your virtues."

The astronomical cost of many films necessitates an audience of such immensity that it makes mediocrity almost compulsory.

There was a time (it was about 1917) when the average cost of a feature (a five-reel photoplay) was about $15,000 to $20,000. It's gone up.

Along with the astonishing inflation of film costs there has been an even more bewildering inflation of executive titles. At the height of his power, when he ran not only MGM but Hollywood itself with the unilateral authority of Hitler, Louis B. Mayer bore the title of vice president. *Vice president!*

Today, as you scrutinize the battalions of vice presidents, senior vice presidents, executive vice presidents, senior executive vice presidents, presidents, vice chairmen, co-chairmen and chairmen which comprise every studio's Table of Organization, you discover that there are no tasks so menial that they are not bespangled with honorifics that would embarrass a banana republic.

There is only one significant title in movie studios: chief executive officer. The rest—whatever it may say on their letterheads—are merely courtiers, in or out of favor, as the case may be.

The term "mogul" is indiscriminately applied by the unsophisticated to virtually every cringing desk-jockey in the studio production department.

A genuinely meaningful definition of the word is "one who can unilaterally buy, sell, hire and fire according to his whim."

By that definition, there are not twelve "moguls" in the entire movie business.

If you were to reject every film proposal made to a studio, you would be correct (from a commercial point of view) nine times out of ten.

Most production executives find these odds impossible to ignore.

The reminiscences of industry veterans are seldom, if ever, reliable. Movie folk tend to place themselves at the center of events to which they were barely admitted, if present at all. They clearly recall being pivotal to the genesis and development of great box office successes and prescient Cassandras of gigantic flops.

I have heard so many preposterous versions of decisions in which I was a participant and/or to which I was an eyewitness—that I have come to regard my *own* recollections with deep distrust!

In 1948, when Louis B. Mayer was toppled from his throne after twenty-four years, his replacement as MGM Studio czar was Dore Schary, a former producer, Academy Award–winning writer and political activist. Schary grandly announced to his friends and well-wishers (there were several thousand of them immediately after his appointment) that he was going to inaugurate a new era at MGM, where the front office would no longer dictate to the back lot, where the imperatives of business would no longer override the aspirations of art. It would be the Golden Age of the writer and director.

It was the sagacious Joe Mankiewicz who alone had the foresight—and the courage—to say to him: "Dore, you have set out to conquer China. In six months you will be Chinese!"

SOCIAL LIFE IN HOLLYWOOD

As Louis Auchincloss characterized Newport society at the turn of the century, social life in Beverly Hills is a random patchwork of borrowed values and recycled opinions—financed on a scale that might embarrass Louis XIV. The monstrous vulgarity which exists at the core of this society is not its ostentation; it is its habit of judging people by standards which have no significant relation to their characters.

The suggestion that any venture into Beverly Hills social life could be described as *climbing* is too fatuous for comment. Spelunking, maybe.

The Talmud teaches that God wants us to perform our charities in secret. This precept has never really caught on in Beverly Hills.

In Africa, the tribal women file their teeth into points, sew pebbles under their skin and distend their necks and earlobes to make themselves more sexually desirable. This is called savagery.

In Beverly Hills, the tribal women chop off the ends of their noses, pump synthetic chemicals into their breasts, extract natural lipids from their buttocks and hack away any dermal extremities to make themselves more sexually desirable. This is called self-improvement.

Naked lust in its pure form is hard to find in Hollywood. Most sexual congress occurs as a transaction involving political, professional or social advantage.

The most intellectually challenging moment of the average Bel Air dinner party arises at its conclusion. You have to go out into the night and find the right Mercedes.

Hollywood, of necessity, is an upstart society, a nouveau-riche society. It is, therefore, ironic that the bitterest competition among these *parvenus* has to do with which of them is the authentic aristocrat.

Taste in Hollywood reflects the eagerness of its *arrivistes* to feverishly acquire and proudly display the time-worn artifacts and trappings of an aristocracy that would have despised them.

I know a successful producer who was more than willing to spend $2 million for a Monet, but who refused to spend two hours in a museum looking at six Monets infinitely superior to the one he bought.

At dinner parties in Beverly Hills, the life of the mind is not a hot topic of conversation.

Haute cuisine is a recurring subject of discussion in Beverly Hills, despite the fact that epicurean tastes and patrician palates are virtually impossible to find there.

In his *Physiolgie du goût*, Anthelme Brillat-Savarin states unequivocally: "Tell me what you eat and I will tell you what you are!"

Hollywood has altered this maxim to: "Tell me *where* you eat and I will tell you *who* you are!"

When Beverly Hills society takes up a new restaurant, we hear much praise and appreciation of the *haute cuisine.* In fact, the quality of the food has little to do with the success or failure of the restaurant. The denizens of Beverly Hills are not looking for a place to eat; they are seeking a venue where famous people congregate in order to be famous together. They find this reassuring. The proximity of other renowned faces serves as a validation of their own tenuous grip on fame.

Thus, the establishment functions not as a temple of gastronomy, but rather as a *fricaterie,* a kind of ego-massage parlor for the chronically insecure.

There are worthy and enterprising citizens in Hollywood who lease premises, install tables and chairs, cook food, and then sell it. This is a perfectly honorable way to make a living. But it does not explain why the practice makes those entrepreneurs —however temporarily—the social arbiters of the film community.

And yet, the importance of these *Berühmtheitkammern* for celebrity hobnobbing should not be underestimated.

There is a widespread impression in Hollywood that if a month goes by and you are not seen at Morton's—or Spago, or Drai's, or Eclipse, or the Grill, or Cicada—it can only mean that you are standing somewhere at a stop signal, holding a large cardboard sign upon which is scrawled the legend: WILL MAKE MOVIES FOR FOOD.

Of course, there *was* a time when much the same mystique glorified Chasen's, and Romanoff's, and Ciro's, and Perino's, and Mocambo, and the Trocadero —and lo, all their pomp of yesterday is one with Nineveh and Tyre!

The freemasonry of fame governs movie-making society.

In the social transactions of Hollywood, celebrity is a negotiable currency. However, as with all currencies, it is subject to the fluctuations of the marketplace.

If you happen to be the media-event-of-the-moment, do not be surprised at the number of total strangers who will eagerly extend warm invitations for you to attend a lavish dinner.

Mme. Verdurin is alive and well and living in Holmby Hills.

And the first thing she will mention is not the *haute cuisine,* but the list of all the other media-events-of-the-moment who are going to be there.

Among the more piquant superstitions of movie-making is the ineradicable belief that failure and success are both highly contagious. This explains the social brutalities which characterize much of life in Beverly Hills.

Gratitude, in Hollywood, is subject to a Statute of Limitations. Fifteen minutes after the benefaction all claims are invalid and no rights can be enforced.

Steadfast friendship is not unknown in Hollywood, but it is rare. Learn to distinguish between genuine fellowship and the dubious cordiality prompted by self-interest.

No matter what name is inscribed in beautiful and careful calligraphy on the envelope, many an invitation to a Beverly Hills dinner party is, in reality, addressed to "Current Office Occupant."

On Rodeo Drive, extortionate price tags and highly publicized labels are frequently mistaken for fashion elegance.

Those of us who relish Hollywood sex scandals would do well to remember that every human being in the civilized world, at some time or other, has done *something* he would prefer not to be caught doing.

HOLLYWOOD MYTHOLOGY

MYTH 1:
IT WAS A SHAME THE STUDIOS HAD TO SELL THEIR THEATERS—THAT WAS THE BIG MISTAKE!

This is the pet myth among those who subscribe to the studiocentric vision of the universe: Hollywood is the hub around which everything else revolves. It is extraordinary how many reputable critics, historians and film authorities simply do not understand that *the major studios never owned theaters. Theaters owned studios!*

Consider the famous aerial shot of the MGM lot over which the sign reads: METRO-GOLDWYN-MAYER STUDIOS. CONTROLLED BY LOEW'S INCORPORATED. *Controlled* is the operative word.

A little history: we can skip over the battle between the Trust (the companies which held the patents on all the camera and projection equipment used in movies) and the Nickelodeon operators to examine how movie studios came into being.

In the early years of the century, the owners and operators of Nickelodeons (who liked to call them-

45

selves "exhibitors") needed films—usually one or two-reelers—to show to their audiences. They *bought* these films from independent contractors. Once the films had been shown, they had no further value to the exhibitors who then brought them to an office called an "exchange" where the films were literally *exchanged* for other films which their audiences had not yet seen. Ultimately, the owners of the exchanges assumed a brokering power—which made them one of the important building blocks in the Exhibition/Distribution/Production Complex.

The "independent contractors" were usually moonlighting theatrical-stage folk—temporarily unemployed actors and stage managers, working under pseudonyms to escape the stigma of turning a buck by working on those lowly immigrant diversions called "flickers" or "movies." Notice that there were no writers (in the technical sense) involved: this was the period when movies were—in Ben Hecht's felicitous phrase—"shouted into existence."

The contractors—actors, a cameraman, and the director (as the loudest shouter came to be known)—would disappear into the park, or the countryside, or the seashore, and return at the end of the day with a movie.

Exhibitors (and later exchanges) would pay these contractors a flat sum ($250 to $500 per reel—very substantial money for 1910 when you could buy a sound house in a decent neighborhood for $2,600). The exhibitor then owned the film outright.

Enter an exhibitor with a brilliant idea. "Hey, fellas," he addressed his colleagues, "why are we paying all this big money to these rumpots and mountebanks and women of doubtful virtue? Why don't we do what Tom Ince did—*hire* them at a modest weekly wage? Then they can make movies *under our supervision*! Instead of one measly movie per day, they can work on two or three *every* day and we only have to pay them for a week's work!"

The logic was irrefutable: the exhibitors opened, or acquired, or acquired and expanded movie studios. They hired—sometimes under contract—actors, directors, cameramen and, oh yes, writers. Writers, you say? Why on earth hire writers? The reason was economic. Exhibitors calculated that if the planned film was *written* (rather than left to the capricious improvisations of the actors and the director) the film could be *budgeted*—and thus be *controlled* by the studio. The system had begun.

With the inauguration of the studio (the word does mean workshop, remember) the exhibitors now had an assured source of product (they love that word). This enabled the store-front Nickelodeon to be magnified into the Motion Picture Palace which evolved, finally, into the mighty chains—Loew's, Paramount, Warners, Fox, Universal, etc.—which defined the *business* of movies for our time. The *art* of film is a separate subject.

After a big theater chain played its own movies in its own theaters, it had reciprocal agreements with the other big theater chains to play off in those areas around the country where it had little distribution.

This was a very cozy arrangement—if you were a big theater chain. If you were a small independent exhibitor, however, you got shafted. You were frozen out of booking the major productions—and lost the large audiences they attracted. You had to live with the Poverty Row productions of Columbia (in *those* days) and Monogram and Mascot and Producers Releasing Corporation.

A number of doughty independents availed themselves of the legal remedies provided by the antitrust and restraint-of-trade laws. They brought lawsuits against the big theater chains. The legal process being then exactly what it is now, the big exhibitors were able to keep those cases tied up—unresolved—stalled—for *over twenty years*!

The theater chains always had the power in the movie business. The theaters kept—through one accounting system or another—roughly eighty-eight cents out of every box office dollar; only about twelve cents went to the studios to defray the costs of production. There was nothing illegal, or even improper, about this arrangement—the theaters owned the studios. It was like deciding which of your pockets you wanted to keep your money in.

Of course, under this system, studio profits were modest, while theater profits were huge. Thus, when Clark Gable requested a raise in salary, it was possible for Louis B. Mayer to explain, with perfect honesty, "My boy, the studio barely scraped by last year!" Gable may have been too tactful to mention that Mayer's yearly bonuses were predicated on Loew's—not MGM's—profits.

And Loew's profits just wouldn't quit. Even in the teeth of the Great Depression, when a few studios (Paramount, Universal) filed for bankruptcy, the movie business as a whole—and Loew's in particular —*thrived!* Movies were the poor man's entertainment; they were depression-proof!

But the day finally came when movies were superseded by television as the poor man's entertainment. And then it was a whole new ball game.

Movie attendance, formerly automatic, became selective—and then downright fussy. It was no longer necessary to change the program every week. Hit movies could run three, four, *six* weeks! To profitably operate a theater chain, it was no longer necessary to make fifty-two pictures a year.

The result? It was no longer *economically efficient* to maintain those sprawling, expensive factories on the West Coast with their extravagant contract lists, their wasteful production practices, their intolerable egos. There were now too many other sources of "product."

So what did the big theater chains do? They remembered those old independent exhibitor lawsuits that they had successfully stymied for decades, and they *consented* to divest themselves of their studio holdings (which they were delighted to get rid of)—the famous "consent decree"—to settle the suits. The studios had no voice in the matter. Their owners, the big theater chains, simply cut the studios loose.

(This began another war—between the studios, who now financed and distributed their own films, and the exhibitors—over the division of the box office dollar. That war continues to this day.)

MYTH 2:
LOUIS B. MAYER WAS AN IGNORANT, VINDICTIVE SON-OF-A-BITCH WHO CONSPIRED TO DESTROY THE CAREER OF JOHN GILBERT OUT OF PERSONAL MALICE!

Circa 25 B.C., the Roman satirist Horace inscribed these lines on a wax tablet: MULTA FERO, UT PLACEM GENUS IRRITABILE VATUM. This translates loosely as: "I put up with a lot to pacify the touchy tribe of poets!"

Horace may not have foreseen the institution of the major motion picture studio two thousand years in the future—but he could not have written a more apt description of the problems with which Louis B. Mayer grappled for almost twenty-five years.

ARS GRATIA PECUNIAE would have been a more appropriate motto for the MGM company trademark than the more familiar one, but even given Mayer's dedication to profit (and the power that came with it), he displayed, over the years, a remarkable capacity for personal loyalty.

Louis B. Mayer was paternal—even patriarchal—and when you have said that, you have said the best of him and the worst of him. He bullied and stormed and tyrannized—convinced that he and he alone knew what was best for his "family." He had rigid notions of what was proper and little tolerance for divergent opinions. But, like fathers before him—and after him—he guided, he nurtured, he protected.

Mayer alienated a lot of people, including some close relatives. He was an easy target for calumny. The boss always is. But his effectiveness as architect and chief administrator of MGM's astonishing growth is unimpeachable.

Herman Mankiewicz (as was his custom) explained the paradox concisely: "Louis B. Mayer is a shit! But not every shit is Louis B. Mayer."

One of the enduring accusations against Mayer is "The Destruction of John Gilbert" story. Eleanor Boardman, an MGM contract player once married to King Vidor (in an interview used in the mini-series *The Lion Roars* as well as in the vastly superior Brownlow-Gill series *Hollywood*), supplies these details: Garbo had failed to appear for her wedding to Gilbert. In the washroom, Mayer attempted to ease Gilbert's despair by advising, "Don't marry her! Sleep with her!" which prompted Gilbert, in a burst of indignation, to strike Mayer, knocking him to the tile floor. From that moment, Mayer vowed revenge! Mayer then conspired with sound technicians to raise Gilbert's voice to a squeaky soprano in his first sound film—and that ended Gilbert's career.

This provocative tale was highlighted by

Gilbert's daughter, Leatrice Gilbert Fountain, in *Dark Star,* her affectionate biography of her father. It was later picked up and embellished by Garson Kanin, in his *roman à clef Moviola.* The account was widely circulated and given ready credence despite its glaring implausibilities.

Is it reasonable to suppose that Mayer was unaware that Gilbert was *already* sleeping with Garbo? Is it reasonable to suppose that Gilbert would consider such a suggestion an insult to the honor of the woman he loved? Come *on*!

Jack Gilbert was intelligent; he was literate; he was convivial; he was a nice guy. But he was *not* a brawler: he was a drinker and a lover.

Mayer, on the other hand, *was* a brawler (a former junk dealer, he had forearms like Popeye). Sam Marx's tale of Mayer vaulting the desk and decking Gilbert, after Gilbert's casual remark that his own mother was "a whore," is entirely consistent with the characters—and the physiques—of both men.

(By the way, *The Lion Roars* does include a number of film clips of Mayer delivering public speeches which should once and for all dispel the notion— much beloved by actors portraying him—that Mayer talked like Jackie Mason.)

Now, anybody who imagines that, in 1929, Mayer (or anybody else) could conspire with sound technicians to alter voices—for ill or for good—doesn't know history. We have the testimony of Margaret Booth, MGM's revered film editor, that Douglas Shearer (Norma's brother), who was put *in charge* of the new sound department at MGM, "didn't know anything about sound." *Nobody* knew anything about sound. The craft was in its crawling infancy.

Then there is the evidence of the Gilbert film itself: *His Glorious Night.* It can be seen on videotape today. It's based on a Molnar stage success (*Olympia*). It was directed by Lionel Barrymore. *And there is nothing wrong with Gilbert's voice!* It's not James Earl Jones's voice, but it is neither high nor effeminate nor is Gilbert a bad actor—far from it.

So, what happened? The evidence suggests that the *kind* of movie—the overblown romantic drama—which had made Gilbert the highest paid star in Hollywood, simply fell out of favor. It happens. No one contends that every faded star in the business is the victim of a conspiracy.

Given the disastrous audience reactions to *His Glorious Night,* as well as the jeering critical reception, it is startling to discover that the film actually turned a profit for MGM—possibly a tribute to the power of a Loew's release or, perhaps, the desire of many to see the train wreck. But both Mayer and Thalberg were aware that Gilbert was in trouble—and they did not just shrug it off. Quite apart from everything else, they had an expensive contract with Gilbert—and, whatever else they may have been, Mayer and Thalberg were not men who broke contracts.

Over the next three years, they starred Gilbert in *seven movies* (eight if you want to count *Queen Christina*), desperately searching for an image for Gilbert which would rekindle his stardom. Three of those stories were chosen by Gilbert himself: he *wrote* one of them! Nothing worked. *Redemption, Way for a Sailor, Gentleman's Fate, The Phantom of Paris, West of Broadway, Downstairs, Fast Workers*— seven consecutive bombs.

Gilbert died, despairing, at the age of forty-two.

Tragic? Of course. But it was not the handiwork of Louis B. Mayer.

MYTH 3:
IRVING THALBERG WAS A WARM, MUCH-BELOVED, MOVIE-MAKING GENIUS—THE GREATEST MOVIE EXECUTIVE OF ALL TIME!

That Irving Thalberg was a genius is an assertion that seems to go unchallenged and unexamined in virtually all movie-making circles. Thalberg's associates, including Mayer, all deferred to his production wisdom. The mention of his name today commands a respect bordering on reverence.

F. Scott Fitzgerald described Thalberg as "the only man who carried the entire equation of motion pictures in his head." Why movie-making is an "equation" rather than, say, a problem in long division remains a mystery. Exactly what is being equated with what?

S. J. Perelman devastated the Thalberg mystique in a piece he wrote titled "And Did You Once See Irving Plain?" Among the statements of Mosaic profundity which Perelman attributed to Thalberg was this gem: "In motion pictures, the writer is a necessary evil."

In all, Perelman provided a thumbnail sketch of Thalberg as a man with a seriously banal turn of mind. Happily for MGM, Thalberg's taste (lower middle-brow) coincided exactly with the taste of the bulk of the movie audiences of the day.

Anita Loos, who worked for Thalberg: "He was not Saint Irving."

The objective evidence would indicate that Thalberg's genius was political—not cinematic. In that respect he was the forerunner of most of today's crop of studio geniuses.

He was certainly a shrewd psychologist. He was often quoted as saying, "This business is so new that nobody really knows anything as a certainty. If you speak with total confidence, people will do it your way. And if they do it your way, no one will ever know if some other way might have been better!"

But what drove Thalberg was the same engine that drove Mayer: money and power. His tolerance for contradiction was smaller than Mayer's—which is to say nonexistent. Thalberg was, in the testimony of his *admirers,* an authentic power freak. You did not last at MGM if you disagreed with Thalberg.

Edward G. Robinson, who declined to work for Thalberg: "It was his way or no way!"

Thalberg was hardly a visionary. Under his leadership, MGM neither pioneered nor innovated. His stated policy was, "Let the other studios experiment. If something works, then we'll do it better." Thalberg's assessment of talking pictures was quoted in all the trades: "A passing fad."

Thalberg's attempts to abort the birth of the Screen Writers Guild were notorious: bribes, intimidation, dismissals, threats of blacklisting, creation of a rival studio-sponsored guild—the whole arsenal of corporate sovereignty.

In the 1934 California gubernatorial campaign, Upton Sinclair, an avowed Socialist, was running as a Democrat against Republican Frank Merriam. Thalberg personally supervised the fabrication of fraudulent documentary shorts (he used footage from *Wild Boys of the Road*) purporting to show thousands of vagrants and bums (that's what they called the homeless in 1934) flocking to California in freight cars to cash in on the Socialist bonanza if Sinclair won. Thalberg then saw to it that these bogus shorts played every theater in the state.

When challenged on the fairness of these tactics, Thalberg replied coolly, "Nothing is unfair in politics." Could James Carville or Mary Matalin have put it more succinctly?

The Thalberg legend will undoubtedly survive intact. Look what he has going for him: his extreme youth, his good looks, his giant success—and, above all, his early death.

Alive, Thalberg was a hated and feared rival to Mayer. Dead, he was the object of Mayer's official canonization. The legend of Thalberg was forged into a weapon with which Mayer beat the crap out of every aspiring executive on the MGM lot. "Irving was like a son to me! Oh, if only Irving were here! None of you are as smart as Irving!" Sidney Franklin, Hunt Stromberg, Larry Weingarten, Joe Mankiewicz, Mervyn LeRoy, Bernie Hyman, Arthur Hornblow, Pan Berman, Sam Zimbalist, Arthur Freed—they all had to listen to that.

Perhaps the definitive verdict on Thalberg's character was delivered by MGM executive Eddie Mannix: "Irving was a sweet guy—but he could piss ice water!"

MYTH 4:
WALT DISNEY CREATED AND DREW
MICKEY MOUSE.

As a matter of fact, he didn't do either.

Walt Disney didn't draw very well—not Mickey, not Minnie, not Donald, not Pluto—not even the familiar copyrighted signature which still appears on screen, in comic strips and in published material. He had people to do that.

There are a half-dozen versions of the story of Mickey Mouse's creation by Disney on a train heading west. There is also a lot of kapok about a pet mouse kept by Disney in Kansas City. There is no substantiation of these fanciful tales whatever. All this information was issued by Disney publicists and sanctioned by Disney himself.

The cold fact seems to be that Mickey (né Mortimer) Mouse was a deliberate knockoff of Oswald the Rabbit, a cartoon on which Disney had worked (and which was, apparently, a knockoff of Felix the Cat). The early Mickey drawings look embarrassingly like Oswald with smaller ears.

And all this knocking off was done not by Disney but by his sometime partner and friend— later, his rival—the now forgotten Ub Iwerks.

Iwerks left Disney to go to MGM where he

produced and drew the unsuccessful series *Flip the Frog*—only to return as a hired hand. Flip, incidentally, looked very much like Felix, Oswald, and Mickey—with no ears at all.

Steamboat Willie, the first Mickey Mouse sound cartoon and the film that skyrocketed Mickey to stardom, carried this informative credit:

A WALT DISNEY COMIC
by UB IWERKS

This credit appeared on the earliest Mickey Mouse cartoons (*Plane Crazy, Gallopin' Gaucho* [originally silent, sound later added], *Steamboat Willie, Mickey's Choo-Choo,* and *Mickey's Follies*). It then disappeared forever—along with the original name of the company once known as Disney Brothers Studio.

From then on, so far as the general public knew, Walt Disney was doing a single.

Make no mistake, Disney was a genius—but not for creation or for drawing. His genius was for organization, for stimulating and motivating people and—the rarest of all—for knowing the real goods when he saw it.

MYTH 5:
THE PIONEER MOGULS WERE SEMI-LITERATE BOORS WHOSE LACK OF EDUCATION AND REFINEMENT VULGARIZED AND DEBASED THE CONTENT AND QUALITY OF THE EARLY FILMS!

This conceit was embraced, enlarged, and embellished by self-styled aesthetes in the first decades of the century.

Stories about Goldwyn, Fox, Zukor, Lasky, Mayer, Cohn, Laemmle, and Warner—their mangling of the English language, their ignorance of classical authors and their unfamiliarity with great literature—were cherished (and amplified and invented) at the Writers Table in every studio commissary. The stereotype was reinforced by a dozen plays and films in which the studio head was thus characterized.

That this assessment was rather self-congratulatory to the writers and aesthetes seemed to go unnoticed.

The moguls' attraction to tawdry material was not based on innate coarseness of taste. It stemmed from sound empirical principles. Vulgarity in a movie is, after all, flattering to the great majority of the audience.

In the old Mutoscope Parlors *The Dance of the Seven Veils* and *Championship Boxing Highlights:*

Johnson vs. Jeffries pulled in a helluva lot more pennies than did *Niagara Falls* or *The Royal Gardens at Kew*. This aspect of the movies, by the way, has not altered in one hundred years.

What most people failed to appreciate then—and now, for that matter—is that the ungrammatical, syntax-torturing, malapropist moguls were closer to the fundamental nature of film than the writers were.

The authentic response to visual stimuli—the cinematic image—is neither linear nor cerebral: it is immediate and visceral. It has nothing to do with literacy or with verbal facility. This sensibility is the *sine qua non* of Hollywood success. Those of the early moguls who had it, prospered; the others disappeared.

And, curiously enough, it remains a sensibility to which a doctorate in English literature is entirely irrelevant.

THE GREATEST LIES IN SHOW BUSINESS

#1   WE HAVE A REALLY GREAT SHOW
      FOR YOU TONIGHT!

#2   HE'S WONDERFUL TO WORK WITH!

#3   BELIEVE ME, I FOUGHT HARD FOR
      YOU, BUT THE STUDIO WOULDN'T
      BUDGE.

#4   BY THE TIME WE GET TO CABLE AND
      VIDEOCASSETTES, WE'LL HAVE A BIG
      PROFIT.

#5   I'LL GET RIGHT BACK TO YOU.

#6   JUST TO BE NOMINATED IS HONOR
      ENOUGH.

#7   THEY OFFERED IT TO ME, BUT I TURNED IT DOWN.

#8   THEY FLIPPED FOR IT, BUT I DIDN'T WANT TO GO WITH A BIG STUDIO— THEY DON'T LET YOU MAKE THE PICTURE YOUR WAY.

#9   I OWE YOU A BIG ONE.

#10   WE SNEAKED IT IN SIOUX CITY LAST NIGHT AND THE AUDIENCE APPLAUDED FOR FIFTEEN MINUTES!

#11   HE GOT TWICE THAT FOR HIS LAST PICTURE!

#12   THIS IS ALL WE'VE GOT IN THE BUDGET.

#13   YOU'RE JUST LIKE FAMILY!

#14 WELL, WE'RE SHOWING TEN DAYS
     OVER SCHEDULE, BUT WE FINISHED
     ALL THE TOUGH SCENES. WE'LL MAKE
     UP THE TIME NOW ON THE EASY STUFF.

#15 I'M A BIG FAN.

#16 BUSINESS WAS A LITTLE DISAPPOINT-
     ING HERE—BUT IT WAS A HUGE HIT
     IN EUROPE, SO NOBODY LOST ANY
     MONEY.

#17 I WAS JUST GOING TO CALL YOU!

#18 THE SCRIPT IS THE MOST IMPORTANT
     ELEMENT IN A MOVIE.

#19 IT'S REALLY GREAT TO BE HERE!

#20 HE WAS ALWAYS OUR FIRST CHOICE
     FOR THE PART.

#21 THE CHARACTERS AND EVENTS IN THIS MOTION PICTURE ARE ENTIRELY FICTITIOUS. ANY RESEMBLANCE TO ACTUAL EVENTS OR PERSONS LIVING OR DEAD IS PURELY COINCIDENTAL.

#22 IT WAS MUTUALLY AGREED THAT HE DEPART THE PROJECT BECAUSE OF CREATIVE DIFFERENCES.

#23 YOU'VE BEEN A WONDERFUL AUDIENCE!

#24 TOM CRUISE IS DYING TO PLAY IT, BUT WE DON'T WANT HIM. HE'S NOT RIGHT FOR IT.

#25 NO OTHER STUDIO HAS SEEN THIS YET.

#26 YOU'RE ON THE SPEAKER-PHONE, BUT I'M ALONE IN THE OFFICE.

#27 THIS IS STRICTLY BETWEEN THE TWO OF US.

#28 I GUARANTEE WE CAN DO IT FOR THE BUDGET.

#29 THIS PICTURE IS GOING TO GET MADE!

#30 I NEVER READ REVIEWS.

#31 THIS INFORMATION CANNOT BE REPEATED OUTSIDE THIS ROOM.

#32 WE WANT TO BE IN BUSINESS WITH YOU! WE JUST HAVE TO FIND THE RIGHT PROJECT!

#33 HE WILL BE MISSED.

HOLLYWOODESE

THEY SAY:
Classics from the Golden Age of Hollywood.

THEY MEAN:
Whatever old movies the TV station was able to buy cheap from the syndicator.

THEY SAY:
It grossed $100 million!

THEY MEAN:
It actually took in $86 million at the box office, of which the distributor received $38 million in rentals, from which was deducted a prints-and-advertising cost of $25 million, leaving a balance of $13 million to defray a negative cost of $40 million plus a finance interest charge of $4 million. They lost $31 million out-of-pocket—and, figuring in the distribution fees paid by the distributors to themselves, the books show a net loss of $43,540,000.

THEY SAY:
Down the line, the picture will show a profit.

THEY MEAN:
We don't want to take the write-off this year.

THEY SAY:
The studio did their usual creative accounting.

THEY MEAN:
We signed a production-and-distribution agreement and now we're pissed-off because the studio expects us to live up to it.

THEY SAY:
Let me think about that. We'll talk tomorrow.

THEY MEAN:
I do not have the authority to make this decision.

THEY SAY:
We want a really great script!

THEY MEAN:
We want a really hot star, and we'll go with any piece of crap he'll commit to!

THEY SAY:
Film is a director's medium.

THEY MEAN:
We want a really hot star, and we'll go with any idiot director he'll approve!

THEY SAY:
I'm going to read this script personally.

THEY MEAN:
It's going to a reader.

THEY SAY:
I can't wait to read it!

THEY MEAN:
It's going to a reader.

THEY SAY:
I'll read it this weekend.

THEY MEAN:
It's going to a reader.

THEY SAY:
I haven't finished reading it.

THEY MEAN:
The reader's report hasn't arrived.

THEY SAY:
I want to reread the script tonight.

THEY MEAN:
I'm going to read it for the first time.

THEY SAY:
Remember this is only a first draft.

THEY MEAN:
It's the fifth draft.

THEY SAY:
Here's the first rewrite.

THEY MEAN:
It's the tenth draft.

THEY SAY:
He's always been very nice to me.

THEY MEAN:
My job depends on the dirty son-of-a-bitch!

THEY SAY:
We're re-releasing it due to popular demand!

THEY MEAN:
The picture we originally scheduled won't be ready in time.

THEY SAY:
The picture scored 98 percent in the two top boxes!

THEY MEAN:
It was a lousy preview.

THEY SAY:
The studio didn't know how to sell it.

THEY MEAN:
The picture is a dog.

THEY SAY:
The new studio head always hated me. And, he didn't want the old studio head to be credited with any hits. So they torpedoed the release.

THEY MEAN:
The picture is a dog.

THEY SAY:
It needs very special handling.

THEY MEAN:
The picture is a dog.

THEY SAY:
It has to find its audience.

THEY MEAN:
The picture is a dog.

THEY SAY:
We don't like this script.

THEY MEAN:
The big star didn't like the script.

THEY SAY:
We like this script.

THEY MEAN:
The big star likes the script.

THEY SAY:
This script needs work.

THEY MEAN:
The big star hasn't made up his mind yet.

THEY SAY:
You couldn't *drag* me to that party!

THEY MEAN:
I wasn't invited to that party.

THEY SAY:
February is a terrific month to open! You're not up against all the big Christmas or summer blockbusters!

THEY MEAN:
The box office prospects of your movie are so dismal, we're not going to waste good playing time on it.

THEY SAY:
I look forward eagerly to my new association with this great studio and I welcome the demands and challenges of this important post.

THEY MEAN:
I got the job.

THEY SAY:
For a long time now I've been wanting to lay aside my executive responsibilities and focus my creative attention on my own independent productions.

THEY MEAN:
I got fired.

THEY SAY:
This town runs on relationships.

THEY MEAN:
This town runs on greed.

ORIGINALITY IN HOLLYWOOD

At the height of the investigation by the House Un-American Activities Committee into the movie industry's entanglements with Communism, Socialism and other subversive philosophies, it was a weary Dorothy Parker who shrugged: "The only 'ism' Hollywood believes in is Plagiarism!"

Mrs. Parker's much-quoted joke was appropriate to its time, but it reveals a certain innocence.

"Plagiarism" is a legal term, subject to a precise legal definition. To appropriate another's work and to pass it off as one's own becomes "plagiarism" (known in the law as infringement of copyright) only when the appropriated work is protected by copyright.

Shakespeare was not *plagiarizing* Plutarch (or Holinshed or Marlowe or Giraldo Cinthio) any more than Arthur Laurents was *plagiarizing* Shakespeare in *West Side Story*.

Mrs. Parker was making a valid point about a lack of originality in Hollywood, but distinctions have to be drawn between plagiarism, remakes, cross-pollination, cribbing and odd coincidences.

Remakes:

The business was founded on remakes. Every studio has recycled a story or plot which it legitimately owns. The usual procedure is to alter the locale, the historical period, the names, the gender of the characters and anything else it can think of to lend a spurious air of freshness to the enterprise.

Paramount's *Sally of the Sawdust* (1925) returned as *Poppy* (1936). Its superb *The Lady Eve* (1941) was mutated into the calamitous *The Birds and the Bees* (1956).

MGM's *The Last of Mrs. Cheyney* (1929) encored in 1937, once more as *The Law and the Lady* (1951). *Lovely to Look At* (1952), memorable only for its total lack of charm, was a watered-down version of *Roberta* (1935). MGM's blah Stewart Granger *Prisoner of Zenda* (1952), made from the same script (and with the same musical score) as the splendid Ronald Colman *Prisoner of Zenda* (1937), is invaluable to film students as an example of how a great script can be screwed-up.

Warner Bros.' *Life of Jimmy Dolan* (1933) reemerged as *They Made Me a Criminal* (1939). *Dawn Patrol* (1930) was remade as *Dawn Patrol* (1938). *The Maltese Falcon* was first filmed in 1931. It was filmed again as *Satan Met a Lady* in 1936. It was not until 1941 that Warners finally got it right with the definitive Bogart-Huston version.

Universal took the swashbuckler *Against All Flags* (1952) which was bad enough, and rehashed it as *The King's Pirate* (1967)—which was worse. It also imagined that its *Beau Geste* (1966) was an improvement on *Beau Geste* (1939), the rights to which it acquired from Paramount.

Twentieth Century-Fox *really* knew how to get mileage out of a story. *Tin Pan Alley* (1940) became *I'll Get By* (1950). *Coney Island* (1943) turned up as *Wabash Avenue* (1950). *House of Strangers* (1949), a taut melodrama about an Italian immigrant family, was revamped as a western in *Broken Lance* (1954), then converted to a circus background in *The Big Show* (1961). *Folies Bergere* (1935), *That Night in Rio* (1941), *On the Riviera* (1951)—three different backgrounds, three different casts, three different sets of songs—and one identical story. *Three Blind Mice* (1938) had more lives than Shirley MacLaine: *Moon Over Miami* (1941), *Three Little Girls in Blue* (1946), and *How to Marry a Millionaire* (1953)—all the same plot.

Cross-Pollination:

The cross-pollination of ideas is part of the creative process in film—as it is in all the arts.

The early animators studied the two-reelers of the great silent comics—less to borrow the occasional idea than to learn *timing*.

The silent comics owed a great debt to English music hall knockabout routines and the *commedia dell'arte*.

The early editors dissected the films of Eisenstein and Pudovkin to learn about montage.

Fledgling directors, even today, run and rerun the films of Griffith, Ingram, Murnau, Ford and Stevens to learn just how much emotional impact the image alone can convey.

All of this is perfectly acceptable—even admirable.

Cribbing:

Cribbing, historically, is part of every artist's tool kit. It is the appropriation of a line, or an idea, or an image—sometimes modified, sometimes not—from another.

George Bernard Shaw cheerfully acknowledged cribbing from Richard Wagner and Oscar Wilde.

You can find cribbing in the Holy Bible (compare II Kings chapter XIX with Isaiah chapter XXXVII).

Robert Aldrich's dolly-shot-along-the-bar in *Four for Texas* (1963) seems to be John Huston's dolly-shot-along-the-bar in *Moulin Rouge* (1952).

The first few minutes of the *Night on Bald Mountain* sequence in *Fantasia* (1940)—Satan with great bat wings perched on a mountaintop, his shadow stealing across the medieval German village—look pretty much like the first few minutes of Murnau's *Faust* (1926).

The scene of the con-man-evangelist-placating-the-hostile-cop-with-a-cold-reading in *Leap of Faith* (1992) reprises the scene of the con-man-spiritualist-placating-the-hostile-cop-with-a-cold-reading in *Nightmare Alley* (1947).

To list the cribs from *Citizen Kane* and *The Maltese Falcon* would require a separate volume.

Odd Coincidences:

Inadvertence plays a major role in all the lively arts. Peter Paul Rubens said that great painting (as opposed to ordinary painting) was the result of "happy accidents."

Coincidences—inadvertent or otherwise—seem to be ubiquitous in the art of movie-making.

Waterworld (1995) looks like *Mad Max* (1979) and *Road Warrior* (1981), but with the cast soaking wet.

Speed (1994) shifts the predicament of *Juggernaut* (1974) from a transatlantic steamship to a city bus.

Ghostbusters (1984) seems an expensive elaboration of the premise of a Walt Disney cartoon called *Lonesome Ghosts* (1937). The parts played by Bill Murray, Dan Aykroyd, and Harold Ramis were played originally by Mickey Mouse, Donald Duck and Goofy.

Sergio Leone's *A Fistful of Dollars* (1964) was belatedly obliged to acknowledge its debt to Akira Kurosawa's *Yojimbo* (1961), but neither film mentioned the patent similarity of their plot structures to the Dashiell Hammett novel *Red Harvest*, first published in 1929.

Uptown Saturday Night (1974) and *Le Million* (1931) both deal with two poor-but-lovable fellows trying to reclaim their winning lottery ticket from the villains who stole it.

Contrast the good-cop-is-the-surprise-villain plot structure of *Legal Eagles* (1986) with *Charade* (1963).

Or, weigh the kidnapped-dignitary-replaced-by-a-double-detected-only-by-the-hero device in *The Prize* (1963) against *Foreign Correspondent* (1940).

See *On the Double* (1961) and then see *Folies Bergere* (1935), not to mention *That Night in Rio* (1941) and *On the Riviera* (1951).

Compare:

- *Only Angels Have Wings* (1939) and *Flight from Glory* (1937)
- *Old Boyfriends* (1978) and *Un Carnet du Bal* (1937)
- *Three Days of the Condor* (1975) and *The 39 Steps* (1935)
- *Red River* (1948) and *Mutiny on the Bounty* (1935)
- *Body Heat* (1982) and *Double Indemnity* (1944)
- *The Big Chill* (1983) and *Return of the Secaucus 7* (1979)
- *Micki and Maude* (1984) and *L'Immorale* (1966)
- *Hardcore* (1978) and *The Virgin Spring* (1959)
- *Ball of Fire* (1941) and *Snow White and The Seven Dwarfs* (1937)
- *Obsession* (1976) and *Vertigo* (1958)
- *Dressed to Kill* (1980) and *Psycho* (1960)
- *Blow Out* (1981) and *Blow Up* (1966)
- *Deathtrap* (1982) and *Diabolique* (1954)
- *Moon Over Parador* (1988) and *Magnificent Fraud* (1935)
- *Switch* (1991) and *Goodbye Charlie* (1964)

The persistent frequency of these coincidences demonstrates the average studio executive's lamentable ignorance of the history of the business that he's in.

Any glib used-car salesman (it has been observed that every major film director has a generous streak of used-car salesman in him) can saunter into a studio executive's office, sit down, spin a wondrous yarn and walk out with a development deal.

The studio executive simply *does not know* that (a) the yarn is not original, (b) it has been filmed before, (c) great (or minor) talents made it and played in it, (d) it failed (or succeeded) at the box office.

This *modus operandi* explains a lot of the eerily familiar movies which get made.

It should be noted that, in recent years, the word *homage* has been pressed into service to account for some of these disconcerting similarities.

It was Peter Stone, writer of the screenplay of *Charade,* who announced one day: "I finally found out what an *homage* is. It's a plagiarism which your lawyer tells you is not actionable!"

AFTERWORD

As a kid, making his hebdomadal pilgrimage to the Saturday matinee at the neighborhood movie house, I knew, instinctively, that the people who acted in movies, and the people who *made* movies, *had* to be the most wonderful and the most interesting people in the world!

As an adult, when a kindly fate had set me down in their midst, I must own that I was in no way disappointed.

If they were sometimes less than wonderful, they were frequently more than interesting!

I found that great film art grows out of the soil of talent and genius—but that it is fertilized with greed, conflict, ambition, vanity, spite, betrayal, doubt, stupidity, deceit and personal jealousy!

So, perhaps, the most valuable thing I learned from my pit-bull is this:

If you can see Hollywood as it is—and still enjoy the work you're doing—if you can see your associates as they are—and still harbor an affection for them—then you *have* succeeded.

"The power of accurate observation is commonly called cynicism by those who have not got it."

—*George Bernard Shaw*